50 classic
cocktails
and lively
libations

party

drinks!

a.j. rathbun

THE HARVARD COMMON PRESS / BOSTON, MASSACHUSETTS

The Harvard Common Press
535 Albany Street
Boston, Massachusetts 02118
www.harvardcommonpress.com

Printed in China

Library of Congress Cataloging-in-Publication Data

Rathbun, A. J. (Arthur John)
  Party drinks! : 50 classic cocktails and lively libations / A.J. Rathbun.
      p. cm.
  Includes index.
  ISBN 1-55832-273-6 (hc : alk. paper)
  1. Cocktails. I. Title.
  TX951.R17 2004
  641.8'74—dc22

                                        2004003285

ISBN-13: 978-1-55832-273-8
ISBN-10: 1-55832-273-6

Book and jacket design by Elizabeth Van Itallie
Photographs by Brian Hagiwara
Styling by Bret Baughman
Props included on pages 4, 16, 29, 59 and the jacket were generously provided by
  Screwpull®, a division of Le Creuset of America, Inc. (www.lecreuset.com)

Special bulk-order discounts are available on this and other Harvard Common Press books.
Companies and organizations may purchase books for premiums or resale, or may arrange a custom
edition, by contacting the Marketing Director at the address above.

10 9 8 7 6 5 4 3

for natalie fuller,
who pours me drinks

table of contents

acknowledgments

My Piña Colada recipe was first printed, in somewhat different form, in the summer 2003 issue of *Tin House*, which you should own.

I'd like to offer up big thanks to my amazing editor, Pam Hoenig, who made this book sing, and to the whole Harvard Common Press crew for all their help in bringing *Party Drinks!* into the world. Thanks times 10 also to my agents, and pals, Rebecca Staffel and Doe Coover, who do a wonderful job. In addition, a large shout-out to my sisters, Holly and Jill, and my mom, Trudy, for teaching me the finer points of throwing parties. Finally, a toast to the amazing bartenders I've had the pleasure of learning from, including Natalie, Jeremy H and Jeremy S, Joel, Ken, Gary and Mardee Haidin Regan, Rich, and the Skoog.

introduction

We are living in a fantastic cocktail era. People at bars and restaurants are enjoying a wide range of inventive new cocktails, as well as rediscovering some dearly missed classic drinks—toasting with friends, family, and sometimes a stranger sitting at the next bar stool. While the reasons for toasting in 20 languages may not have changed much in the past 100 years, what we actually drink has been refined, retooled, and modernized. Perhaps more than at any other time in history, due not only to advancements in the distilling process but also to those in the shipping process, it's possible to get orange-flavored rum in Washington, single-batch bourbon in Florida, and raspberry vodka in Maine almost year round. It's also easier to get fresh lemons, limes, cherries, and many other types of fruit all over the world not long after they've been harvested.

It's a crying shame, though, to have creative cocktails only at bars—with the right recipes and tools it's easy to move the cocktail party into the home or onto the patio. Most great drinks are easy to construct on the kitchen counter, eliminating any reason to stay stuck in that same old drink-making rut when you decide to throw your next party. Whether you're hosting a black-tie winter ball or just kicking it in cutoffs on the deck, a drinking "centerpiece" or two makes the occasion memorable—and takes a lot of the stress off your shoulders. As a host, having a couple of good drinks ready to pour equals a lot less worrying. Though the celebratory instinct is something everyone possesses, throwing a really good gathering can be an undertaking. If you're going to make the effort, why not do it up in memorable style? For example:

"Come over for the annual backyard hoedown, celebrating spring on our balcony. We'll be letting the Horsefeathers loose this Friday at 7:30, and then we'll be rounding them up and drinking them down. Plan on watching the sunset, picking and grinning, and putting your feet up." Now *that's* an invitation that dials in straight to the imagination of any hot-blooded partygoer.

Election results finally in? Then it must be time to have your Democrat and Republican friends over to drown their sorrows and mend their burned bridges over some Kentucky bourbon–based Presidentials (page 46) or, to get really patriotic, American Champagne Cocktails (page 44). It's August and the mercury's risen too high to have people over for yet another sweaty summer barbecue? You'd better transform it into a tropical morning affair and serve up fresh bubbly Mimosas (page 34). Football season's in full swing, but the ubiquitous backyard kegger is not only done to death, but also boring? Go past fourth and long for the six-point score by serving up some Shandy Gaffs (page 49), spiraling that beloved beer into an animated masterpiece with the well-measured aid of one of any home bartender's best friends, ginger ale.

Assembling a gathering around cool party drinks consistently makes occasions more memorable. Achieving it isn't hard; all it takes is some simple preparation, reliable recipes, and good guests.

Of course, the basic idea of serving alcoholic beverage at parties isn't new—it's almost as old as humankind. Like many life-changing inventions, the discovery of alcohol-based beverages probably was accidental: some lucky ancestor of ours mistakenly ate a fermented fruit or grain product and became fond of the taste as well as the effect. I'm guessing many Neanderthals and their descendants convened around the fire, or on the first rocky front porch, with a glass (or a carved coconut) in one hand and friends all around. Our ancestors liked to party, which is why soirées, revelries, bashes, events, festive fêtes, celebrations, casual carousing, mighty merriment, box socials, and just plain parties don't go in and out of style—the love of fun and community is too deep. This deep love of festivity is also why a mundane drink should never be served. It dulls not only the palate, but also the occasion.

picking these party drinks

The drinks in this book are especially tailored to helping put the pizzazz in your next gathering. I selected these particular drinks, classic and new, because each has a bit of sparkle, a sense of suave silliness, and at least an ounce of panache—things needed to make a mundane party mighty. Of course, I also believe they all taste good. This is important, because you don't want to serve a drink that sounds neat-o, but tastes yucky. That won't make your party memorable—or it will, but not in a good way. Finally, a party drink shouldn't be outlandishly hard for the home bartender to construct—otherwise, you (as host or hostess) don't have enough time to actually *enjoy* your party, which would be a crying shame.

While rigorously testing many, many drinks (the sacrifices I've made for you, dear reader) in order to decide which should be included in this volume, I kept in mind all of the above requirements. And also, always, I tried to determine whether I would want to serve the drink in question at a shindig I was throwing. The recipes that remain meet every party standard (whether they've been around for centuries or a few short years) and are truly worthy of being called party drinks.

So kick up your heels, ring up friends and family, and get those party drinks popping!

party drinks
basics

Years ago, along with takeout veggie chow mein, I received one of my favorite fortune cookie fortunes: "Proper prior planning prevents poor performance." As a host, it is a perfect phrase to remember when you're having six people over in 10 minutes and haven't yet thought of what drinks to serve—perfect because you can tell yourself that, next time, you'll remember that fortune and plan ahead.

Planning is a vital ingredient to throwing a hoedown, shindig, or your basic revelry, though, on the flip side, last-minute decisions to have a party in half an hour often lead to memorable occasions (usually at 2 a.m.). I realize that to many, last-minuting is as appetizing as eating Velveeta, but trust me, being impetuous can be fun. Whether you're someone who sends out invitations six months, two weeks, or five minutes ahead of time, having a few essential tools around makes the role of host much easier.

liquors

Your bar essentials are what you're going to build upon, so make sure that you're comfortable not only serving, but also imbibing, drinks made with them.

Six key "base" liquors make the world go round: gin, vodka, rum, tequila, whiskey/bourbon, and Champagne (some might argue over the latter—but ignore those confused folks). It's not a bad idea to always have three around, to cover the party bases and to be prepared for variables in your guests' tastes. Whether you plan a party around one drink or 20, it's polite to be ready to accommodate a drinker who can't tolerate what everyone else is tippling.

Serious home bartenders have their own storage rules and like to debate whether or not to chill certain items. Obviously, Champagne should be chilled before using, but the other base liquors don't necessarily have to be chilled. If you're someone who enjoys any of the clear liquors straight or on the rocks, then I do suggest chilling them (I'm thinking of gin, vodka, and white tequila), in which case there's less need to shake them with ice, which will end up adding a little extra H_2O to the glass.

After the base liquors, there are numerous options when filling out the nooks and crannies of the cabinet. My advice is to settle on a couple of drinks from this book for your next soirée, then pick up the needed non-base liquors (provided you already have the base liquors on hand) from a local liquor store. Repeat this formula for a number of parties in a row (you sure don't want to stop at just one), and soon you'll be able to put together numerous tasty liquid treats at a moment's notice.

mixers

The "mixers" category is broad, enveloping everything from cream to juices to ginger ale and other bubblies, and more. Though many mixtures are man-made, the watchword is "fresh." If a recipe calls for lime juice, squeeze it right before the drink is made for maximum flavor. If a recipe uses ginger ale, don't fall back on an old opened bottle that's been in the fridge for weeks (ginger ale, club soda, and their ilk do not get better with age). The bottle, when opened, shouldn't give a flat *pfumpf*, but instead speak out with a mighty carbonated hiss. Also, if the cream's been sitting next to the mustard for a month, that Alexander isn't going to end the formal dinner party with anywhere near the proper note. You get the idea. Mixers are important to every cocktail, so don't take them for granted.

Beyond the "fresh" rule, there are a few other mixer considerations. While mixers may not seem as important as top-shelf booze, you should not skimp on them. Using a cut-rate ginger ale or club soda may keep a few extra pennies in your pocket, but it could easily destroy a whole party by changing the drink flavor from fantastic to fatal. Also, unless a recipe specifically mentions "seltzer" instead of club soda, don't substitute one for the other. Club soda's mild base tends toward larger bubbles, and you'll miss them if they're not around. Of course, if you have an old-school soda water dispenser (which are sometimes called seltzer dispensers), call me and we'll use it together. One final mixer concern: though tonic water isn't used in many cocktail recipes (due to its ability to take over the flavor of a drink), it's not a bad idea to have a good brand-name bottle on hand, as lots of folks love the basic gin and tonic.

While the above mixers may be used in larger amounts, there are some secondary mixers that absolutely make a drink shine. First and foremost are fruit juices (these are often the primary mixer in a drink, too). As mentioned above, "fresh" is the key to any fruit juice. If you don't have a juicer, and can't procure one at the present, it is *possible* to use frozen juice as a mixer—but always be sure to have some fresh fruit around to use for garnishing and to add a tang of freshness.

When buying fruit, pick those that are unbruised, shiny with rich color, and exhibit a tiny bit of give to the skin when they're squeezed. Don't be afraid to handle fruit in the store—just smile while doing it. Avoid fruit with large jaundiced areas or visible brown ridges, which point to a sourness that is definitely not a home bartender's friend. To get the maximum amount of juice, it's best to have fruit at room temperature. If you've been storing it in the fridge, you can pop it in the microwave wrapped in a damp towel for about 20 seconds or give it a soak in some warm water. Also, roll the fruit under your palm, exerting steady pressure, before juicing. You'll kick up your heels at how much juice you get.

Another essential that is mixed into many drinks is bitters. Bitters is a distillation of numerous secretive ingredients, including herbs, spices, roots, and more. There are presently two chief bitters varieties available, Angostura and Peychaud, though there used to be many and it's still possible to find orange, mint, and other flavored bitters (a company called Fee Brothers is the place to start). Angostura and Peychaud bitters are very different in flavor and in how they interact with a drink, so it's best not to interchange them. Angostura is much earthier, with a stronger flavor that really intensifies a cocktail; Peychaud is more flowery in taste, a little lighter, and tends to iron out a cocktail's edges a bit. Bitters will keep for quite a while in a cool cabinet, so there's no reason not to stock both.

There is one more secondary mixer that *must* be mentioned, and it can break the "fresh" rule a little. That hallowed mixer is simple syrup. Simple syrup is your pal, the kind of pal that you'll like having around, pre-made, before the party. I tend to always have a partially full bottle in the fridge (in an old Orange Crush bottle, to be exact) with a pourer on it—just to be primed, as so many cocktails utilize simple syrup. Making it is fairly undemanding, using the following recipe.

simple syrup

Simple syrup will keep, tightly covered, up to a week unrefrigerated and up to a month refrigerated.

2 cups water
3 cups granulated sugar

1. In a medium-size saucepan, combine the sugar and water. Bring to a boil over medium-high heat and continue to let boil, stirring, until the sugar has dissolved.
2. Remove the pan from the heat and let cool completely.

MAKES 4 CUPS

ice

Ice plays a part in almost every drink (except the warm ones, of course). Because of this, you'll want fairly fresh ice, as ice exposed to too many odors will taint the drink. For most shaken drinks and drinks served over ice (on the "rocks," if you will), use standard 1-inch ice cubes. These are large enough that they won't completely disappear in a drink. But if your only cubed ice has been living in the freezer since the '80s, buy cracked ice, which is the kind regularly sold in grocery stores. Its irregularly sized pieces may melt a bit quicker, but work better than stinky cubes. Also, cracked ice is always used when making certain mixed drinks that benefit from a little extra H_2O. If you can get it, using block ice in punches is attractive, and once in a while shaved ice is a treat (there are specialty ice shavers that will do the trick nicely). Crushed ice, which is the smaller ice often seen in fountain drinks, is the choice for slushier drinks such as daiquiris. You can facilitate your own crushed ice by giving some cracked ice a quick spin in your blender.

gilding the lily

It's crucial to remember that in most cases, even after the drink has been shaken or poured or ladled, it's not quite done. The right garnish tops off both the taste and the style of many drinks. With that in mind, it's a smart idea to have a working knowledge of how to construct the basic citrus garnishes: twists, slices, wheels, and wedges.

Twists are probably the most difficult to make and also the most maligned (due to too many bartenders cutting them too small and just dropping them into drinks without actually twisting them). The first step is to make a straight cut across one end of the fruit, cutting off just enough to create flat surface. Then place the fruit, flat side down, on a cutting surface. Using your garnishing knife of choice, cut off ½-inch-wide strips of peel, top to bottom, getting just a bit of the inner white pith and all of the outer skin. Don't forget that after you've used a fruit's skin for twists, the fruit itself is still juiceable; there's no need to waste good fruit juice. Also, don't forget to twist the strip over the drink before adding it to the drink— the light oils that will be released because of that action are crucial.

Wedges are a little easier than twists, and wheels are almost self-explanatory. For the former, first cut the ends off (about ⅛ inch is good). Then cut the fruit in half lengthwise. Lay each half fruit side down on your cutting surface, then make three lengthwise cuts, creating three equally sized pieces. Many drinks also use fruit quarters, which are the just-mentioned wedges cut in half. For wheels, simply cut about an ⅛ inch off each end of your fruit. Then (carefully) cut your fruit into uniform wheels. If you cut the wheels in half, you've got slices.

It's not a bad idea to prepare the above garnishes before the party starts—no host wants to spend party time cutting fruit (and having sticky hands). The key is not letting the fruit dry out. Once it's cut, store it in a damp paper towel in the fridge until you're ready to use it. Just don't let it sit for more than a day, or you'll start losing flavor.

But creative garnishing doesn't begin and end with citrus fruit—there are also mint sprigs, strawberries, raspberries, nutmeg, maraschino cherries, and more. Again, remember the "fresh" rule. There's nothing quite as pitiful as making a mint julep with wilted mint, and even those bottled sweet maraschinos start to smell a little funny if left in the fridge for many months. So treat your garnishes right—you'll reap the rewards.

bar tools

When assembling the home bar tool assortment, a single item shines like a beacon at the top: the cocktail shaker. Though not every drink in this book utilizes a shaker, enough do that you'll be limited without one. There are two options, and both work dandy. The first is what's known as the cobbler shaker. The cobbler shaker has populated cocktail dens since before Prohibition. Most are all metal (18/10 stainless steel assures long life and little staining) and consist of a sizeable bottom piece covered by a top that contains a built-in strainer and a small cap. Cobbler-style shakers are amazingly easy to use and allow the home bartender to jump right into concocting without fear. Just add the ingredients to the larger bottom piece, secure the top, and shake. Then remove the cap and strain into glasses.

The Boston shaker—our second shaker type—may take some time to master, but also delivers lovely chilly results. It consists of a glass bottom cup and a top cup made of metal. Once the ingredients are added to the bottom cup, invert the metal cup into the glass. Then, using the palm of your hand (and a bit of care), thump the bottom of the upside-down metal shaker. This should create a seal between the two pieces. Then get to shaking, being sure to hold both pieces *securely*, one in each hand. Once the drink is shaken, place the shaker on a flat surface, metal side down. Strike the metal piece with your hand again to break the seal. After that, use a strainer to pour the drinks into glasses. Whichever shaker type you bring home, I suggest shaking drinks for between 10 and 15 seconds on most occasions (if a drink needs a longer or shorter shake, the recipe will instruct as such).

It might seem odd to call a pitcher a bar tool, but for throwing parties at home, the description fits. I like to have at least two pitchers around, one that's a little fancier and one that's a little sturdier. I use the prettier one for inside get-togethers only, because outside things are bound to get bumped around. It's a good idea to have a pitcher with a pouring lip, for two reasons. First, it obviously makes pouring easier, and second, it makes it easier to keep ice from leaving the pitcher—this being helpful when you're mixing drinks with ice in the pitcher, but pouring them into glasses that don't need extra ice. Glass pitchers are always nice, but ceramic, china, and porcelain ones also stand out. Good bar pitchers range in size from a small 50 ounces up to 100 ounces. When a recipe mentions a large pitcher, you need one that holds 75 to 100 ounces.

After the shaker and pitcher (or pitchers) are secured and installed on a shelf of honor, the next pieces of the home bar puzzle are a jigger for measuring (get one that has a 1-ounce measuring cup on one side and a 1½-ounce cup on the other) and a muddler. The muddler is a wooden instrument used to macerate and mix items in the bottom of a glass or shaker. Shaped much like a small baseball bat, a muddler should be slightly bulbous at one end (the muddling end) and sturdy. Avoid those with any sort of varnish, as it'll end up in the drinks (which doesn't contribute anything nice). If you can't find a muddler, have a designated hearty wooden spoon around as a substitute.

so what exactly is an ounce?

Just in case you don't have a jigger or other bar measuring device, it's a good idea to familiarize yourself with some basic conversions:

1 fluid ounce = 2 tablespoons
8 fluid ounces = 1 cup
1 quart = 4 cups or 32 ounces

These should allow you to make most drinks with measuring spoons (let's hope it doesn't come to that) should you find yourself jiggerless. And consider yourself formally warned: If you don't have a jigger, but picked up a souvenir shot glass on vacation in Vegas, don't just guess that one shot glass equals an ounce (or any specific measurement). Most shot glasses aren't regulated, so always test first before using one as a measuring device. ("Testing" it doesn't mean throwing back a shot and seeing whether you think it feels like 2 tablespoons in your mouth; pour a shot, then measure it.) Many cobbler-style shakers now come with a top "cap" that can double as a measuring device; just read the box to be sure how much it holds.

A fourth fundamental tool is a sharp, maneuverable garnishing knife. A good paring knife works, provided the blade isn't too thick. It doesn't hurt to have a longer utility knife close at hand also, to slice larger fruit such as mangos and to keep greedy hands away from the maraschino cherry supply.

You might also want to invest in a solidly constructed electric blender. Look for one that has multiple speed settings and a pulse feature. Often when working with ice you'll need to start slowly before moving into crushing speeds. Be sure your blender has stainless steel blades and that all parts can be removed easily for cleaning. Go for a model that holds at least 40 ounces. A slight pouring lip on the blender's pitcher is also nice, but only if the lid seals tightly around it. In the recipes, when it calls for a medium-size blender, you'll need one that holds at least 27 ounces. When a large blender is called for, you'll need one that holds 48 ounces.

Other prime bar tools include a thin, long bar spoon for stirring up drinks, a corkscrew, bottle openers, a handheld spice grater (for nutmeg and citrus zest), and brightly colored sparkly swizzle sticks and stirrers— 'cause every bar needs style and color.

In addition, there exist a number of bar tools and bar accompaniments that may not seem as necessary, but which come in handy. These include an ice bucket (that doesn't leak) and ice scoop, bar towels and cutting boards, coasters or cocktail napkins, measuring cups and spoons, and a glowing party attitude, brought out to cover spills.

glassware

While having a line of glassware that runs for miles and includes not only a poco grande glass but also a pousse-café glass is snazzy, it can drain the pocketbook and fill the counter space. There are, however, several glassware mainstays that will cover a lot of ground, starting with the cocktail or martini glass. This classic stretches from 4 to 12 ounces and features a design known worldwide. The tall, thin, and sleek highball glass (holding 10 to 12 ounces) and its sturdier, squatter cousin the old-fashioned glass (sometimes referred to as a rocks glass) are next on the list. Old-fashioned glasses come in two sizes, the regular, which runs from 6 to 10 ounces, and the double, 10 to 15 ounces. Unless otherwise mentioned, if a recipe calls for an old-fashioned glass, the regular size is what is meant. For hot drinks, it's a good idea to invest in some sturdy, heatproof mugs—a set of glass mugs is nice. In addition, if you like larger drinks (especially those with a beer base), it's a good idea to keep a couple of 24-ounce beer glasses, what are known as "big girls," chilling in the freezer. Rounding out your fundamental glassware collection should be a set of basic white- and red-wine glasses (with the red being a balloon-like goblet) and a set of sparkly Champagne flutes.

While I'm not a fan of serving drinks in plastic cups, neither do I leave a party if that's what's being offered. A drink won't taste as good in plastic (it always has a hint of plastic odor) and it's a bit wasteful, but I can understand how great big gatherings might put the fear of breakage into a host or hostess. Just be sure never to serve a hot drink in a plastic cup (unless, of course, you actually want to see an unmitigated disaster), and never, ever serve a martini in anything but glass. That's worth a spanking.

party drink math 101— scaling recipes up or down

As good parties depend on having friends or a significant other around, almost all of the drink recipes in this book are designed to make more than one drink. I know (believe me) that parties can unexpectedly shrink or expand—that's one of the characteristics that makes them fun—so I've made a special note on the few drinks that don't readily scale up or down. Many drinks do, though, as long as the ratios between the ingredients stay the same. If it's 2 parts liquor A plus 1 part mixer B, keep it that way, no matter how many ounces A and B equal.

a final toast

The bar is stocked, the essentials are in place, and you've shined your shoes and buckled your buckles. What's next? Read on and get out of that old cocktail rut. Whether celebrating the first 90° day, a first date, or the first night in a new house, once you whip up a party drink, any basic run-of-the-mill celebration transforms into a dolled-up special occasion remembered far longer than breakfast the next day. These drinks squeeze like a lime wedge over dull evenings, making entertaining more enjoyable, while making it easier to throw a successful, memorable party. Don't wait any longer—pick up the phone, call some friends, and let the party begin. Cheers! Bottoms up! *Skål! Na zdorovie!* Here's to you!

party
animals

T here are cocktails, and then there are the classics that populate this chapter. These liquid idols have been served in the living room, lounge, and backyard for many years, earning their high-ranking places in the drinker's pantheon. Passed down through generations of festive gatherings, they add a hint of history and more than a shaker's worth of class whenever they're served. True party animals, they're always in fashion and always ready to get that soirée started right.

blood and sand

Doesn't this venerable quaff sound dangerous and itchy? And the ingredients at first glance may seem a mistake—how could they combine without destroying the stomach? But don't back away in fear—it's actually a little sweet, though packing quite the kick. I suggest serving it on Halloween, or maybe during an annual scary movie festival.

Ice cubes
3 ounces Scotch
3 ounces cherry brandy
3 ounces sweet vermouth
3 ounces orange juice
Orange slices for garnish (optional)

1. Fill a cocktail shaker half full with ice cubes. Add all the ingredients, except the garnish, with a scowl. Shake well.
2. Strain the mix into 4 cocktail glasses. Garnish each with an orange slice, if desired. Drink. Modify scowl to smile.

SERVES 4

"ALWAYS CARRY A LARGE FLAGON OF WHISKEY IN CASE OF SNAKEBITE AND FURTHERMORE ALWAYS CARRY A SMALL SNAKE."—W.C. FIELDS

bloody mary

The Bloody Mary is a hazardous drink—not necessarily in the traditional sense, but because most bartenders and party-givers are absolutely positive that their recipe is the only one true way to concoct this breakfast favorite, and anyone who disagrees is in for trouble. Start with the following recipe as a touchstone, then adapt it as needed or wanted.

Ice cubes
6 ounces vodka
8 ounces tomato juice
2 ounces fresh lemon juice
2 dashes Louisiana-style hot sauce
2 dashes Worcestershire sauce
$\frac{1}{2}$ teaspoon celery salt
Salt and freshly ground black pepper to taste
Celery stalk, or pickle, or pickled green bean for garnish

1. Fill a medium-size pitcher half full with ice cubes. Add the vodka, juices, hot sauce, Worcestershire, and spices. Stir well.

2. Fill 2 pint glasses three quarters full with ice cubes. Carefully pour the mix equally into the glasses.

3. Garnish each glass with a celery stick and serve.

➤ A Variation (well, actually, several): A couple of quick ideas to try are reducing/increasing the hot sauce/Worcestershire sauce components; adding 1 teaspoon prepared horseradish; omitting the celery salt entirely; and/or adding a whole jalapeño to each glass as a garnish.

➤ A Virgin Variation: Some don't want to start *too* early in the morning. To make a Virgin Mary, substitute an additional 5 ounces tomato juice and ½ ounce fresh lemon juice for the vodka.

SERVES 2

A NOTE: I like a tall vertical garnish in a Bloody Mary. However, many enjoy a squeeze of lime or lemon, so you might want a plate of lime and lemon wedges as alternative garnishes. Whatever makes people happy makes for a happy party.

mai tai

Start pouring Mai Tais and any afternoon turns into a humid paradise—just break out the grass skirts and tiki torches. This drink is traditionally shaken and served as a single, but I'm not fond of wearing grass skirts solo, so I tend to make them by the pitcher so as to get every guest into the tropical mood without having to wait. This Tahitian favorite features orgeat, a sugary almond-flavored syrup that can be found in gourmet food stores or bar supply stores.

Ice cubes
10 ounces dark rum
4 ounces orange curaçao
4 ounces fresh lime juice
1$^1/_2$ ounces orgeat
Lime wedges and fresh mint sprigs for garnish

1. Fill a pitcher three quarters full with ice cubes.

2. Add the rum, curaçao, lime juice, and orgeat to the pitcher. With a very sturdy spoon, stir vigorously for about a minute. While you're doing this, have the other guests set up the limbo pole and the tiki torches.

3. Pour the mix, ice and all, into four 10-ounce glasses. Garnish each glass with a lime wedge and two mint sprigs. Now, start shaking that grass skirt.

➤ A Variation: If your pitcher is big enough, you can add 4 ounces fresh orange juice to the mix and call it a Suffering Bastard. But I wouldn't try it in polite company.

SERVES 4

daiquiri

This storied sultry favorite has been sung about enough—what more can be said except that its ideal combination of savory rum, tart lime, and sweetness makes one heck of a poolside companion—when served in a glass, of course. But Daiquiris don't talk much, so you'll want to invite a posse of pals over and make a pitcher full. If you don't have an actual pool to congregate around, pull the bathtub into the yard and take turns soaking. Though they often get made in a blender, I think Daiquiris are best stirred with ice, instead of smashed. Using crushed ice gives it a nice slushy feel.

Crushed ice
12 ounces light rum
6 ounces fresh lime juice
3 ounces Simple Syrup (page 13)
Lime wedges

1. Fill a pitcher with crushed ice. Add the rum, lime juice, and simple syrup, and stir well.

2. Pour into 6 highball glasses (or cocktail glasses, if you're feeling fancy). Squeeze a lime wedge over each glass, dropping the wedge into the glass once it's squeezed. In case of rain, add a tiny umbrella to each glass if available.

➤ A Variation: If watermelons are in season, why not a Watermelon Daiquiri? First (and do this the day before you're drinking), halve the watermelon. Then, using a small ice cream scooper or melon baller, scoop out a dozen or more round pieces of watermelon, trying to avoid including any seeds. Put these in the freezer overnight and stick the remaining watermelon in the refrigerator. The next day, spoon out 1 cup of the flesh, removing any seeds, and run it through the blender until it liquefies (a couple of seconds). Add 6 ounces of this watermelon "juice" instead of the lime juice to the above recipe. Once you've poured the drinks, garnish with a lime wedge (squeezing it, as indicated above) and 2 or more frozen watermelon balls. Eat the rest of the watermelon in your favorite style.

➤ A Virgin Variation: When making Virgin Daiquiris, it's probably a good idea to go the strawberry route, as lime virgins don't offer a lot to sip on. Substitute 5 ounces strawberry syrup for the rum, increase the simple syrup to 6 ounces and the lime juice to 8 ounces, and garnish with 6 chopped strawberries. Stir well, adding cold water if needed to thin.

SERVES 6

long island
iced tea

This spring break (and general beach-living) darling is known almost as much for its powerful thump as for its actual good tea taste. It's a drink that makes you wonder, "Does there really need to be a cocktail that contains five serious liquors?" But when the temperature soars above 90° and sand and surf and sun tease you into bikinis and bathing trunks, there's no denying that a Long Island goes down smooth and cold.

Ice cubes
3 ounces vodka
3 ounces white tequila
3 ounces white rum
3 ounces gin
3 ounces triple sec
3 ounces Coca-Cola
1 ounce fresh lemon juice
Lemon slices for garnish

1. Fill a large pitcher three quarters full with ice cubes. Add the vodka, tequila, rum, and gin, 2 at a time (as if the pitcher were the Ark). Add the triple sec last, as it's slightly afraid of swimming. Give the mix 1 stir with a long spoon.

2. Add the Coca-Cola and lemon juice. Stir briefly.

3. Fill 4 highball glasses halfway with ice. Add the mix. Garnish with lemon slices.

SERVES 4

A WARNING: Needless to say, the Long Island Iced Tea is a walloper. Be careful when drinking, as its friendly taste disguises its potency. "One is nice, two is okay, three is a problem" is a good rule for all guests at a Long Island party.

bronx cocktail

The Bronx is charismatic enough that it's an ideal drink for watching baseball, for accompanying breakfast, and for adding a needed buffer when the
in-laws show up unexpectedly. Just start stirring, pouring, and smiling. The
key is to use fresh-squeezed orange juice. You'll be sad for weeks if you use
frozen. To get the conversation started once the drinks are poured, bring up
the fact that the Bronx wasn't named for the borough, but actually originated
at the Bronx Zoo. You'll seem smart and talented.

Ice cubes
6 ounces gin
3 ounces sweet vermouth
3 ounces dry vermouth
6 ounces fresh orange juice (from about 2 good-sized oranges)
Orange slices for garnish

1. Fill a medium-size pitcher half full with ice cubes. Add all the ingredients, except the garnish. Stir well with a syncopated rhythm.
2. Pour the mix carefully into 4 cocktail glasses, making sure no ice
makes the trip. Garnish with orange slices. When serving, remind folks about
how good orange juice is for you. It's like you're drinking vitamins.

SERVES 4

"THEY ALL THOUGHT SHE WAS
DEAD; BUT MY FATHER HE KEPT
LADLING GIN DOWN HER THROAT
TILL SHE CAME TO SO SUDDEN
THAT SHE BIT THE BOWL OFF THE
SPOON." —FROM *PYGMALION*, BY
GEORGE BERNARD SHAW

margarita

The Margarita, without question, is one of the most popular and badly mixed drinks currently ordered from Florida to Fairbanks. Who created the original margarita? There are multiple possibilities. The first comes courtesy of Margarita Sames, a well-off Texan who, they say, invented the drink during a series of raucous parties or one memorable Christmas party. Next, the romantic version has Danny Negrete, a bartender from somewhere in California, fashioning a drink for his girlfriend, Marjorie (an Americanized version of Margarita). Finally, the working-class version has a nameless bartender creating the Margarita in the 1930s in at local tavern in Mexico. The confusion is the bar: was it was Bertha's Bar in Taxco, the Caliente Racetrack Bar in Tijuana, or the Garci Crespo Hotel in Puebla?

Whichever version you believe, be sure to serve your Margaritas up cold, by the pitcher, accompanied by crisp chips and some spicy salsa.

Crushed ice
12 ounces white tequila
6 ounces Cointreau or triple sec
4½ ounces fresh lime juice
Coarse kosher salt
Lime wedges for garnish

1. Fill a medium-size pitcher three quarters full with crushed ice. Add the tequila, Cointreau, and lime juice. Stir briefly.

2. Pour a small layer of kosher salt onto a small plate or saucer. Take each cocktail glass and wet the outside of the rim with a lime wedge. Holding a glass by the stem, rotate the rim through the salt. You want to be sure that salt coats only the outside of the rim.

3. Once each glass has been salted (unless you have a guest who desires no salt, of course), fill them with the mix. Try to not get any ice into the glass—the drink should be sufficiently chilled from the stirring. Garnish each glass with a wedge of lime.

➤ A Virgin Variation: While Virgin Lime Margaritas are possible (removing the tequila and triple sec and adding orange juice will make a drinkable mix), Virgin Strawberry Margaritas are a better chilly treat. Instead of tequila and triple sec, add 6 ounces fresh orange juice, 4 ounces strawberry syrup, 2 cups sliced fresh strawberries, and a little more ice, and blend until smooth.

SERVES 6

the martini

There are classic drinks, and then there is The Martini. William Powell, playing cocktailing detective Nick Charles in *The Thin Man*, said, "The important thing is the rhythm. Always have rhythm in your shaking. Now a Manhattan you always shake to fox-trot time, a Bronx to two-step time, a dry Martini you always shake to waltz time." I would hate to disagree with Mr. Powell, but I like Martinis stirred, not shaken, and like to make up a pitcher at a time so everyone gets going at once. As Mr. Powell tended to have a pitcher of Martinis around at least once a movie, I don't think he'd mind. (As an aside, a fun party game is to screen any *Thin Man* movie and try to match Nick and Nora Charles—Powell and Myrna Loy—drink for drink. Yowza.) There is one trick to making Martinis by the pitcher: be sure it has a pouring spout. You'll need it to hold back the ice.

Ice cubes
12 ounces gin (or vodka, if you play that way)
2 ounces dry vermouth
Cocktail olive or lemon twist for garnish

1. Fill a pitcher three quarters full with ice cubes. Add the gin and vermouth. Stir well. Carefully pour the mix—making sure no ice gets past, using your stirrer if necessary—into 4 martini glasses.
2. Garnish each drink with a cocktail olive or a lemon twist as personal preferences demand.

➤ A Variation: To make your Martinis dirty, substitute ½ ounce olive juice for ½ ounce of the vermouth. Garnish each drink with 3 olives.

➤ A Second Variation: If you add a cocktail onion as your garnish, you've got a Gibson.

➤ A Holiday Variation: There are now numerous Martini-monikered cocktails, some good, some not so hot. But a Cranberry Martini is easy to make, lovely to look at, and tastes divine. To the above recipe, add 2 ounces unsweetened cranberry juice cocktail to the pitcher along with the gin and vermouth. Before pouring, add 2 or 3 frozen cranberries to each glass. The lemon twist sings well in this cocktail Christmas carol, but leave the olives on the condiment shelf for this one.

➤ A Popular Relation: I would be a very bad host if I didn't mention here the Martini's almost-cousin—the chic Cosmopolitan. To adjust the above recipe for making Cosmos is easy. Just use vodka instead of gin, and substitute 1 ounce Cointreau and 1 ounce cranberry juice cocktail for the vermouth. Garnish with a twist of lime.

SERVES 4

piña colada

The Piña Colada is a group drink (even if it's a group of two). When the temperature's rising and the sun beats down hard, call up a posse and get the blender whirring. This recipe isn't overly sweet, but it does have some of that sticky cream of coconut, so be careful on the countertops. If you don't have dark rum, you can make it with all light rum, but it won't be quite the same. You'll only feel like you're in Miami, and not on an actual island. If the heavy cream is making your heart go pitter-patter a little too heavily, substitute soy milk.

4 cups crushed ice
4 ounces light rum
4 ounces dark rum
7 ounces cream of coconut, such as Coco Lopez
4 ounces heavy cream
16 ounces pineapple juice
Pineapple wedges and maraschino cherries for garnish (optional)

1. Add the ice to a large blender.
2. Pour all the remaining ingredients into a blender, except the garnishes, and blend until smooth, about 15 seconds.
3. Pour mix equally into four 12-ounce glasses. (If you happen to have special poco grande glasses—a 12- to 13-ounce stemmed glass with a wave-and-a-half bowl—use them and listen as your praises are sung.)
4. Garnish with pineapple wedges, if using. If you really want to get the party rolling, garnish with pineapple wedges and a cherry.

➤ A Variation: I'm not sure it's possible to tire of Piña Coladas, especially in summer, but if this dreaded event does happen, try a Strawberry Piña Colada. Reduce the cream of coconut to 3½ ounces and the pineapple juice to 8 ounces and add 3½ ounces strawberry syrup and 1 cup hulled and chopped strawberries. You could also garnish each glass with a slice of fresh strawberry or a whole one, if that's your pleasure.

➤ A Virgin Variation: To set up a Virgin Piña Colada, drop the rum completely and add an extra 2 ounces pineapple juice per drink.

SERVES 4

mimosa

The Mimosa is a breakfast and brunch favorite. Others may enjoy a Bloody Mary, but it's too heavy for some to approach before noon. The Mimosa, on the other hand, is airy with citrus undertones—fizzy sunshine in a glass. Could there be a better way to start off the day than with friends, fruit, and Champagne? No matter how scruffy you're feeling, a Mimosa makes the day's outlook brighter, especially if it's a Saturday or Sunday and you're seated around a table on the deck or in a well-lit corner of the kitchen. There are few things finer in life.

8 ounces fresh orange juice
One 750-milliliter bottle chilled Champagne
Orange slices for garnish

1. Add 2 ounces orange juice to each of 4 Champagne flutes.
2. Fill each glass with Champagne. Garnish each glass with an orange slice.
➤ A Variation: Once, upon waking with a desire for mimosas, I found myself deficient in orange juice. But I did have a nice fresh mango. Before long, I was serving Mango Mimosas to a happy crowd. The key was "juicing" the mango. First, peel it; then cut the chunks of flesh off the pit. Next, puree the chunks with a ½ cup water in a food processor. Once it's reached a fairly smooth and pourable consistency, you're set. Follow the recipe above, substituting mango juice for the orange juice. The results are destined to add a little tropical flavor to your morning.

SERVES 4

tequila sunrise

The Tequila Sunrise (Kurt Russell movies aside) features a sweetness that can shift to sugary without the right hand at the controls. When serving them to a group of friends or family, don't get distracted—you must be navigator behind the home bar, as well as captain. Of course, you get to be the first one to taste the drinks, so it's not all heavy sailing.

Ice cubes
8 ounces tequila (Tequila Nacional is nice, but any clear tequila will work)
16 ounces fresh orange juice
2 ounces grenadine

1. The first move is to pour 2 ounces tequila into each of 4 highball or comparable glasses filled with ice cubes. Your tequila should be chilled—if not, fill a shaker with some ice and add the tequila, then strain it over the ice in the glass.

2. Add 4 ounces orange juice, slowly, to each glass. Mix the two—gently.

3. This is the crucial step—the adding of the grenadine. This not only determines whether your drink will taste good, blending the citrus, sugar, and tequila into a fine cocktail, but also adds the visual aspect to the drink. Some say the best way is to tilt the glass and pour the grenadine very quickly into it, but I find this leads to oversweetening. Instead, put a pourer onto the grenadine bottle (make sure it has a small opening), then leak out a little while keeping the bottle at a right angle to the glass. You'll want to move the bottle around the glass's circular top and won't want to be pouring for more than a few seconds.

SERVES 4

ward eight

The Ward Eight is a fantastic discussion drink—serve it at one of those more "refined" parties when you're having only a couple of friends over to talk through the events of the day. The drink's history goes back to Boston in 1898, when it was created at the Locke-Ober restaurant to celebrate the election of one Martin Lomasney to the state legislature (Martin was from the Eighth Ward). Of course, after a couple you may want to stop talking and dance on the table. Which is fine, too.

Ice cubes
4 ounces rye (or bourbon, if you're rye deficient)
2 ounces Simple Syrup (page 13)
1 1/2 ounces fresh lime juice
1/2 ounce grenadine
Orange slices and maraschino cherries for garnish

1. Fill a cocktail shaker half full with ice cubes. Add the rye, simple syrup, and lime juice. Shake rapidly.
2. Add the grenadine and give it another quick shake.
3. Strain everything into two 5- to 7-ounce stemmed goblets or other comparable stemmed glasses.
4. Garnish with an orange slice and cherry, unless you're morally opposed.

SERVES 2

A NOTE: Unlike many of the drinks in this book, this one is measured for two, for two reasons. First, when having an evening of intellectual drinking, it may be nice to have only a couple of invitees. Second, you would have to have a rather large shaker to make four Ward Eights at once, and I would hate for you to spill any of it. If you do want to up this mix to four, just double the amount of each ingredient. But be careful of the grenadine; you don't want to oversweeten this.

drinks that
refresh

W Whew, it's hot out. And tropical temperatures, my party friends, demand a drink that not only lightens the soul but also helps to balance out all that sun. Luckily, this chapter's selections are designed to cool things down a bit while kicking the party up to the next level. Serve them up whenever that mercury starts to rise, whether it's morning, noon, or just past sunset. It's never too sultry for a party, as long as you're serving the right refreshing cocktail.

- Horsefeather
- Lime Rickey
- Black Velvet
- American Champagne Cocktail
- Dublin 8
- The Presidential
- Orange Buck
- Shandy Gaff
- Pimm's Cup
- Sloe Comfortable Screw
- Summer Beer
- Fuzzy Navel
- Sweet Press
- Tequila Cocktail

horsefeather

When you start to sweep off those back porches, verandas, balconies, decks, and terraces, or mow the backyard and bring the lawn furniture out of the basement storage area, it's time to get on the phone, call 15 or so of your closest friends whom you haven't seen since the sun went south for the winter, and tell them you're opening the gate to let the Horsefeathers loose. Of course, they might think you're crazed with a case of spring fever, but once you enlighten them to this deliciously light bourbon cocktail, they'll not only show up at your door, they'll also probably develop a little "spring fever" of their own.

Ice cubes
12 ounces fine Kentucky bourbon (Maker's Mark is nice)
One 2-liter bottle ginger ale
8 dashes Angostura bitters

1. Place a good 6 ice cubes in each of 4 highball glasses.
2. Add, nice and slowly, with a steady hand, 3 ounces bourbon to each glass. Top off with the ginger ale.
3. Add 2 shakes of Angostura bitters to each glass—if you have to use another bitters, it'll do in a pinch. Stir well.
➤ A Variation: If the idea of a drink named "Horsefeather" seems a little too fluffy as you sit out viewing your imagined back 40 acres, there's an easy remedy. Get your trusty zester/stripper and take a few long peels off a lemon. Before even adding ice to the glasses, drape a spiral strip of lemon onto the edge of each glass—then proceed with the above directions. You'll be drinking a Horse's Neck.

SERVES 4

lime rickey

Always start an evening or afternoon that is to be spent drinking Lime Rickeys by telling your guests, "Rickeys go way back," mysteriously. Then start mixing the drinks and say nothing else about it. If anyone asks you, later, what you meant, you could tell them how the Rickey was invented near the end of the nineteenth century for a colonel who later became a major lime importer. But me, I like to keep the mystery. This recipe sometimes goes by the plainer moniker of Gin Rickey. I think Lime Rickey sounds, well, better. But the choice is yours.

> 3 ounces fresh lime juice (from 2 limes; reserve the juiced halves)
> Ice cubes
> 6 ounces gin
> One 2-liter bottle club soda
> Lime wedges for garnish

1. Divide the lime juice between 4 highball glasses. Add 1 of the lime halves to each glass.

2. Fill each glass three quarters full with ice cubes. Add $1\frac{1}{2}$ ounces gin to each glass.

3. Top off each glass with club soda. Give each drink a quick stir (for your guests' sake, don't overstir). Garnish with lime wedges. Serve with a grin.

➤ A Variation: No gin in the house? Try the Rickey with vodka. It'll do the trick.

➤ A Virgin Variation: A Virgin Rickey, like the original, makes a fine, refreshing sipper. Instead of the gin, add 1 ounce Simple Syrup (page 13) to each glass.

SERVES 4

A NOTE: If you have individual stirrers for each guest, don't be shy about adding a stirrer to each drink.

black velvet

This smooth-sounding and smooth-tasting pour brings the black tie into the pub. The mix of Champagne and stout equals a bubbling dark delight. Serve it either while watching serious sports or at an after-dinner affair that needs loosening up. I know dedicated dark beer quaffers shudder at chilling stout, but for this it must be cold. Trust me.

Two 12-ounce bottles cold stout or other dark beer
24 ounces chilled Champagne

1. Add 6 ounces stout to each of four 12-ounce beer mugs or other 12-ounce glasses.

2. Slowly, carefully, very carefully, add 6 ounces Champagne to each glass. With a stirrer or bar spoon, slowly stir each glass once and serve immediately.

SERVES 4

A WARNING: If you pour the Champagne hastily, or stir too aggressively, expect a mess. And don't call me to clean it up.

american
champagne
cocktail

I first heard of this drink from one of my favorite bartenders, Jeremy Holt, who is also the publisher/editor of *The Husky Boy*, a small 'zine devoted to food and drink. While there are a number of cocktails that employ the bubbly, I'm not sure another manages to combine what at first glance seem such disparate elements: Champagne and bourbon. But don't be scared—the bourbon doesn't overwhelm the light, breezy Champagne; instead, it adds the right amount of smolder and kick, making this an ideal drink both at breakfast gatherings and evening events. You may want to use a mid-range Champagne in this drink, as a premium might be a bit of a waste. But the choice is yours.

Ice cubes (optional)
16 ounces Champagne, chilled
6 ounces orange juice
4 ounces bourbon
Orange slices for garnish

1. Add 1 ice cube to each of 4 champagne flutes. (If your Champagne and orange juice are both well chilled, feel free to skip this step.)
2. Add 4 ounces Champagne to each flute, then 1½ ounces orange juice.
3. Gently float 1 ounce bourbon on top of each glass and mix lightly. Garnish each glass with an orange slice and serve.

SERVES 4

"IN VICTORY, YOU DESERVE CHAMPAGNE, IN DEFEAT, YOU NEED IT."
—NAPOLEON BONAPARTE

dublin 8

The Dublin 8 is spot on for a stylish St. Patrick's Day celebration. While the great pagan-converting saint might have his doubts about the melee enjoyed in his name, I have to believe he would have appreciated the Dublin 8, especially on those days when being a bishop was a little much (talk about a stern boss). I first became acquainted with this drink via Jeremy Sidener, longtime bartender and manager at the venerable Louise's Bar in Lawrence, Kansas. As the story goes, he was talking to a lovely Irish lady in the month of March and decided to create a drink for her right there on the spot. Consider it a green beer alternative as you plan St. Pat's festivities, or any late winter or spring cocktail hour.

8 ounces Irish whiskey (Bushmills is a nice idea)
12 ounces fresh orange juice
12 ounces ginger ale
Ice cubes
1 lime, quartered
Lime slices for garnish (optional)

1. Pour the whiskey into a 40-ounce pitcher.
2. Add the orange juice and ginger ale, together if possible, so they can meet and greet each other before they start mingling with the whiskey. Some may say making this much effort is a little obsessive. I would say that those people have lost their grasp on what's really important in life.
3. After you've added the juice and ginger ale, add ice cubes until the pitcher is full.
4. Pour into highball glasses, making sure to get ice and drink in each. Squeeze a lime quarter over each glass, dropping it in the glass once it has been squeezed. With a long stirrer, whisk the ice around in the glass twice.
5. Garnish with a lime wedge, if you like, but be careful of over-liming.

SERVES 4

A WARNING: While this cocktail has, in essence and ingredients, the spirit of St. Patrick's Day, I am not sure it has ever been made in Dublin, or even Ireland. So when you visit the Emerald Isle, be prepared to instruct your bartender as he or she mixes his or her first Dublin 8.

the presidential

Late January and early February are historical times for enjoying cocktails, because of the prestigious events that deserve toasts. (A full disclaimer is in order: besides those events mentioned, my birthday does fall in early February.) January features inaugurations of new presidents and other national leaders; February boasts birthday celebrations for two of our most revered presidents, George Washington and Abraham Lincoln, as well as President's Day proper. It is only fitting, then, to have a drink meant specifically for these occasions, one that matches them in dignity, but also has the strength of character to keep us warm in the cold months that continue on outside the window while we are raising our glasses inside around the fire.

> 8 ounces Simple Syrup (page 13)
> 8 ounces fine whiskey (Kentucky bourbon is nice, and awfully politician-like)
> 1 ounce fresh lime juice
> Ice (I prefer around 5 good-sized cubes each, but crushed ice also works, and shaved ice might make you look a little dashing)
> Lime slices for garnish

1. Divide the simple syrup between 4 double old-fashioned glasses or other 10- to 12-ounce tumblers. (You should be thinking squat, sturdy, and wide mouthed when picking out the glass for this drink.)

2. Add 2 ounces whiskey and ¼ ounce lime juice, gently, to each glass, as if you were pouring for the president and wanted to demonstrate your ability to be calm under fire.

3. Add ice to each glass and mix with a stirrer, again, gently. Garnish with a slice of lime.

4. Sip slowly, taking time to inhale before drinking—you'll notice how the wide glass mingles the lime and whiskey scents.

SERVES 4

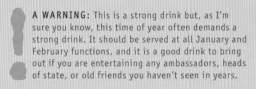

A WARNING: This is a strong drink but, as I'm sure you know, this time of year often demands a strong drink. It should be served at all January and February functions, and it is a good drink to bring out if you are entertaining any ambassadors, heads of state, or old friends you haven't seen in years.

orange buck

One dragging summer, a few co-workers and I decided during a particularly dull afternoon to figure out how many days old we were. It turned out that I was nearing, just weeks away from, my 10,000th day. There must be a culture—my guess is it's currently undiscovered—where the 10,000th day is celebrated. For me, the first step was picking the right libation for the party. That was the Orange Buck, which has become one of my favorite summer drinks. It's light, refreshing, and subtly citrusy, with ginger accents.

> Ice cubes
> 12 ounces gin
> 6 ounces fresh orange juice
> 6 ounces ginger ale
> Lime wedges

1. Fill four 8-ounce highball glasses three quarters full with ice cubes. Add 3 ounces gin to each glass.

2. Add 2 ounces each of orange juice and ginger ale to each glass, at the same time, so neither liquid feels slighted.

3. Stir each glass briefly. Squeeze a lime wedge over each glass, dropping the wedge in the glass after it's been squeezed. Garnish with another lime wedge.

➤ A Variation: If you're feeling rummy, substitute rum for the gin and you're sipping a New Orleans Buck. Feel free to sing the jambalaya song.

SERVES 4

A NOTE: The key, of course, for making these is in the ratios. Use as big a glass as you feel comfortable with, but keep the ratios intact and the Buck won't disappoint. So for every 2 parts gin, you'll want to use 1 part ginger ale and 1 part orange juice.

ANOTHER NOTE: Be warned. Folks drinking multiple Orange Bucks tend toward phrases like "Buck you" and "That's bucked up." Sure, it's childish. But still fun.

shandy gaff

This drink dates back at least to Dickens's era, and probably even further. It's gone through various permutations (such as the question of whether or not to hyphenate "Shandy" and "Gaff"), but the basic building block, beer, has always been a central part of the equation. The beer base is what makes this a supreme concoction for taking your next tailgate or Super Bowl party to a higher level.

One 6-pack amber ale (12-ounce bottles or cans)
One 2-liter bottle chilled ginger ale

1. Pour beer into six 24-ounce beer glasses until halfway full.
2. Fill each glass to the top with ginger ale.
➤ A Variation: If the amber ale doesn't make the meal for you, try the Shandy Gaff with Guinness or another stout beer (keeping the ratio of 1 to 1 between beer and ginger ale) and you've got a Guinness Shandy.
➤ Another Variation: I've heard tell of using lemonade instead of ginger ale in a Shandy Gaff. Feel free to try it out, but don't invite me. I'm sticking with the g-a.

SERVES 6

A NOTE: If you don't happen to have 24-ounce beer glasses, then use pints or other beer glasses. You won't use a full bottle for each drink—just be sure to go half and half, beer and ginger ale.

pimm's cup

My first Pimm's Cup experience occurred in the U.K. (which is nice, since that's where Pimm's is "made to James Pimm's original recipe, a closely guarded secret known only to six people"). I was 14—drinking laws are more relaxed overseas—and hooked to the running-spring-in-a-glass taste as well as intrigued by a drink garnished with a cucumber.

Ice cubes
8 ounces Pimm's No. 1 Cup (a readily available gin-based, slightly fruity liqueur)
One 2-liter bottle ginger ale
Peeled cucumber slices for garnish

1. Fill four 12-ounce glasses three quarters full with ice cubes. Add 2 ounces Pimm's No. 1 Cup to each of them.

2. Top off each glass with ginger ale. Garnish with a cucumber slice.

➤ A Variation: While I appreciate and love the above recipe, I cannot in good faith fail to tell you that freshly made lemonade substitutes for the ginger ale with equally tasty results. At the Napoleon House bar in New Orleans (one of the world's finest bars), they mix a lemonade-style Pimm's Cup. You could do worse things than spend a sunny afternoon there in the back garden, downing a few Pimm's Cups. If using lemonade, add a lemon slice to each glass along with the cucumber.

SERVES 4

sloe comfortable screw

Certain drinks induce a happy grin before the first drop touches the lips. Luckily, this drink doesn't have just a coy name—it tastes good, too, combining two liqueurs that aren't as inviting when taken separately. And think of the fun you'll have making, and others will have reading, invitations to a Sloe Comfortable Screw Party. Be careful sending those invitations at the office, though—you don't want any trouble. The sloe gin featured in this recipe is actually a liqueur made from steeping or crushing sloe berries in gin.

> Ice cubes
> 4 ounces sloe gin
> 4 ounces Southern Comfort
> 16 ounces fresh orange juice
> Orange wheels for garnish

1. Fill 4 highball glasses with ice cubes. Add 1 ounce sloe gin and 1 ounce Southern Comfort to each glass. If you're using new bottles of the liqueurs, be sure to introduce them before adding them to the glasses. It is their first date, after all.

2. Add 4 ounces orange juice to each glass. Stir the drinks in a friendly manner.

3. Garnish with an orange wheel.

➤ A Variation: If you'd like to jazz things up a bit, use 12-ounce glasses and top each drink with 2 ounces club soda.

SERVES 4

summer beer

Summer entertaining opportunities are almost endless: from backyard barbecues to pool parties to watermelon feasts on the porch. After waiting for so long (even in the sweaty South, people dream of summer—it's a holdover from school days, when we all had summer vacations to think about), after weeks or months of winter and teasing spring, summer descends.

Ah, the heat of summer. It gets so hot, how could we possibly plan an enjoyable party with something that refreshes both body and spirit? Well, let me suggest that it's all in pouring a long, tall Summer Beer for each guest. Regarding the beer, it must be an American-made lager: Miller High Life, Budweiser, etc.

> Ice cubes
> 40 ounces lemonade (you can use canned, if the kids on the corner aren't
>   out selling)
> Four 12-ounce cans or bottles beer
> 6 ounces chilled vodka
> Lemon wedges for garnish

1. Set out four 23- or 24-ounce beer or cooler glasses. If you have the room, chill the glasses in the freezer before making the drinks.

2. Add ice (a good-sized handful of cubes), then 9 ounces lemonade to each glass.

3. Slowly add 12 ounces beer to each glass.

4. If you didn't pay attention and added the beer quickly (not slowly), clean up the counter where it bubbled over. Next, add 1½ ounces vodka to each glass.

5. Add 1 more ounce of lemonade to each glass. Garnish with a lemon wedge (you can squeeze the wedge over the glass if you desire).

SERVES 4

NOTE: After the second round has been served, be prepared for many renditions of songs having to do with summer—but with "Summer Beer" inserted. Examples include "Summer Beer, makes me feel fine" sung to the tune of "Summer Breeze" by Seals & Crofts, "The Summer Beer, came blowing in" to the tune of "Summer Wind" by Frank Sinatra, or even "Summer Beer, had me a blast" to the tune of "Summer Nights" by Olivia Newton-John and John Travolta.

fuzzy navel

This cocktail may hearken back to high school (at least it was a favorite at Smokey Valley High School, where I learned to drink), but it tastes good beyond any ability to generate nostalgia. This isn't to shy you away from serving it at your next high school reunion (you should), but don't limit it only to that—it's peachy for other parties, too, and isn't a hassle to make.

Ice cubes
8 ounces fresh orange juice
8 ounces peach schnapps
4 ounces vodka (if you can find peach-flavored vodka, grab it)
Peach or orange slices for garnish

1. Fill a medium-size pitcher half full with ice cubes. Add the orange juice, schnapps, and vodka. Stir well.
2. Fill 4 highball glasses with ice cubes. Pour the mix carefully into the glasses. Garnish each with a peach or orange slice.

SERVES 4

"WE DON'T WANT DOUGHNUTS, HONEY BUNS, POPPY CAKES, AND OTHER DAINTIES; BRING US A WHOLE SHEEP, SERVE A GOAT AND FORTY-YEAR OLD MEAD! AND PLENTY OF VODKA . . . NOT WITH RAISINS AND FLAVORINGS, BUT PURE FOAMING VODKA, THAT HISSES AND BUBBLES LIKE MAD." —NIKOLAI GOGOL

sweet press

Many of life's great pleasures are simple (I believe my grandfather once said), including sleeping in when you're supposed to be at work and then taking the TV out on the back porch in the middle of summer to watch an afternoon baseball game with a cold Sweet Press beside your chair. Luckily, it's so easy to make that you can refresh your drink between innings.

Ice cubes
8 ounces gin
6 ounces club soda
6 ounces 7-Up or Sprite
Lime wedges for garnish

1. Fill a large pitcher half full with ice cubes. Add the gin.
2. Add the club soda and 7-Up simultaneously. Stir rapidly with a bar spoon or other long spoon for 5 seconds.
3. Serve in highball glasses garnished with a wedge of lime.
➤ A Variation: Feel free to go the vodka route (instead of gin)—it's also lovely. And if just lime's not quite fancy enough for your back porch, add a sprig of fresh mint to each glass.

SERVES 4

tequila cocktail

There's no denying it—I'm a tequila fan of substantial proportions. And I'm not alone. Though I love to sip well-chilled top-end tequila solo, and could swill simply perfect Margaritas for hours, it's also good to expand one's tequila horizons by mixing it in other cocktails. The following is an uncomplicated recipe that doesn't take away from tequila's naturally complex flavors.

Ice cubes
1 ounce fresh lemon juice
1 ounce fresh orange juice
1 ounce Simple Syrup (page 13)
4 ounces white tequila
Orange slices for garnish

1. Fill a cocktail shaker half full with ice cubes. Add the juices, simple syrup, and tequila. Shake vigorously.

2. Strain equally into 2 cocktail glasses. Garnish each glass with an orange slice.

➤ A Variation: Want to give your Tequila Cocktail a bit more of a kick and a little glamour? Substitute Grand Marnier for the orange juice and call it a Top-Shelf Tequila Cocktail.

SERVES 2

drinks that
impress

Whether you want to pour an exceptionally pretty cocktail to sweeten up that special someone or you have a need to set up quaffs for four with an extra-special flair, the drinks here are sure to impress. A little style, a dash of pizzazz, and that added ounce of *oh yeah*, topped with fresh mint, frozen raspberries, or a simple sliver of strawberry, make these favorites memorable—and ensure that your party will always be remembered.

- Peach Bowl
- Red Carpet
- French 75
- Alexander Cocktail
- Caipirinha
- Silk Stocking
- Kir Royale
- Mint Julep
- Mojito
- Flowered Wine Spritzer
- Gin Stinger
- The Rebecca

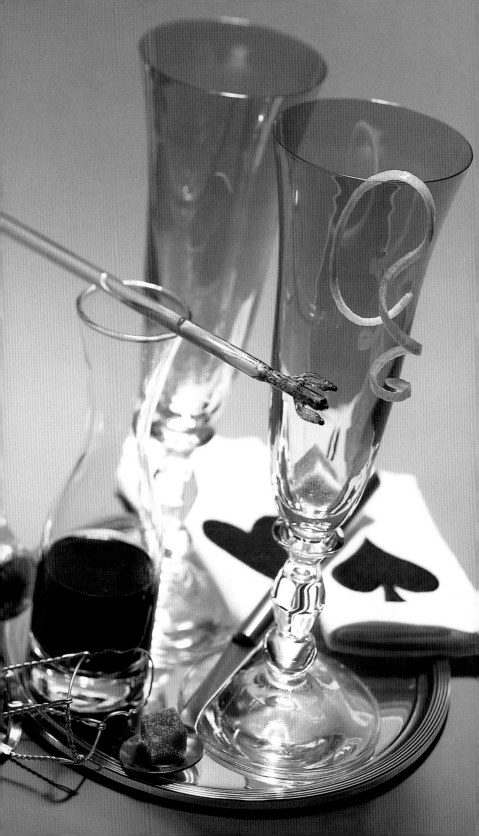

peach bowl

I first picked up this fruity special from Patrick Gavin Duffy's *Standard Bartender's Guide* (revised by the venerable James Beard, no less). It sports an eye-grabbing presentation and tastes, well, peachy. It's a great centerpiece drink for any occasion when fresh peaches are in season.

4 small fresh, ripe peaches, washed well and left unpeeled
One 750-milliliter bottle chilled Champagne
Thin peach slices for garnish (optional)

1. Make 4 slices with a sharp knife on two sides of each peach. You'll want to make clean cuts, but they don't need to be too deep.

2. Place a peach in each of 4 wide goblets.

3. Fill the goblets with Champagne and garnish each with a single peach slice, if desired.

➤ A Variation: Peaches not in season, or not at the market? Try this with strawberries instead, adding 3 or 4 to each goblet (depending on the size of the strawberries), for a Strawberry Bowl.

SERVES 4

A NOTE: If these Bowls don't have enough fruit flavor for you or your guests' tastes, add $1/2$ ounce chilled peach schnapps to each goblet before the Champagne.

red carpet

Though it can be treacherous to taste buds to invent drinks on the spot, it can conversely lead to memorable results (and, it's a kick). This drink was born from this type of instantaneous creation during a sluggish afternoon. It was just days before the Academy Awards and a friend of mine had planned a considerable award-watching party, but didn't know what to serve as a signature cocktail. She wanted something with flourish, something that matched the dressed-up occasion while recognizing some of the night's inherent silliness. The resulting drink fit that bill, and she rolled out the Red Carpets all night.

Ice cubes
6 ounces gin
3 ounces sour cherry syrup
One 2-liter bottle orange-flavored club soda
Orange slices and maraschino cherries for garnish

1. Fill a cocktail shaker half full with ice cubes. Theatrically add the gin and sour cherry syrup. Shake well.
2. Add 2 ice cubes to each of 4 highball glasses or other tall, thin glasses. Strain the mix equally into the glasses.
3. Top off each glass with club soda. Garnish each with an orange slice and a cherry (two cherries for anyone who knows who won Best Actress in 1953 for *Roman Holiday*).

SERVES 4

A NOTE: If, sadly, you aren't able to track down a bottle of sour cherry syrup (try a gourmet food store before despairing), switch to 2½ ounces grenadine and ½ ounce fresh lemon juice. Just don't tell anyone from the media.

ANOTHER NOTE: If the convenience store down the block refuses your requests for orange-flavored club soda, you can use regular club soda, but add ½ ounce fresh orange juice to the shaker with the gin and sour cherry syrup.

french 75

Oo la la. This drink sings of cosmopolitan parties (or, as the French say, *le partee*) and hearkens back to days when the continent was reachable mainly via an extended boat trip. Of course, it features Champagne and demands a fashionably large garnish. Whether you wear a beret when serving it and fake a French accent is completely up to you.

Ice cubes
2 ounces fresh lemon juice
2 ounces Simple Syrup (page 13)
4 ounces gin
One 750-milliliter bottle chilled Champagne
Lemon and orange slices for garnish
Maraschino cherries for garnish

1. Fill 4 highball glasses three quarters full with ice cubes. Add ½ ounce lemon juice, ½ ounce simple syrup, and 1 ounce gin, in that order.

2. Top off each glass with Champagne and garnish with a lemon slice, orange slice, and cherry (you can use a toothpick to attach the garnishes together, if desired). Serve each drink with a thin chic straw for stirring and sipping. Also, top each drink with a cocktail umbrella if you want to go Riviera style.

➤ A Variation: If 75 doesn't seem enough for your occasion, substitute brandy for the gin. Then you've moved to a French 76.

SERVES 4

alexander cocktail

It's nice to have a sweet drink in your repertoire (or at least to have the ingredients ready in your liquor cabinet or booze drawer), and the Alexander is a scrumptious cocktail to serve with desserts, chocolate, and strawberries. Since it uses cream, it's not going to take off any pounds, but remember that shaking a cocktail is a form of exercise. It all balances out.

Ice cubes
3 ounces gin
3 ounces crème de cacao
3 ounces heavy cream
Strawberry slices for garnish (optional)

1. Fill a cocktail shaker half full with ice cubes. Add all the ingredients, except the garnish. Shake well.

2. Strain the mix into 2 cocktail glasses. Garnish each with a strawberry slice, if desired.

➤ A Variation: If you substitute brandy for the gin, you've got a Brandy Alexander (fancied by grandmothers worldwide).

➤ A Second Variation: If you substitute crème de menthe for the crème de cacao, you've set up an Alexander's Sister Cocktail. Fun, isn't it? I would skip the strawberries with Alexander's Sister—she doesn't play well with fruit.

SERVES 2

caipirinha

This Brazilian beauty has reached "all-the-rage" status over the past few years, crossing the country quicker than a spilt drink spreads over a counter. The Caipirinha (pronounced ki-pea-REE-nya) utilizes cachaça (say KUH-shah-suh), the national liquor of Brazil (not surprisingly, the Caipirinha is the national drink of Brazil). Cachaça, which is distilled from sugar cane, is becoming easier to find in liquor stores, which means there's no time like the present to have your own at-home Carnival—just slap on some samba music, pour some Caipirinhas, and start swinging. The following version is for six, because you can't samba alone.

4 limes, quartered, plus more quarters for garnish
6 tablespoons light or dark brown sugar
Cracked ice
12 ounces cachaça

1. Place the lime wedges and brown sugar in a medium-size pitcher and muddle them together well with a muddler or large wooden spoon, making sure the limes release most of their juices.
2. Fill the pitcher with cracked ice, add the cachaça, and stir well, until the sugar is completely dissolved.
3. Pour the Caipirinhas, lime wedges and all, into 6 sturdy old-fashioned glasses, making sure each glass gets ice as well as drink. Garnish each glass with two lime wedges.
➤ A Variation: If you can't find cachaça, you can substitute vodka. Then you're drinking a Caipiroska (I'd still samba).

SERVES 6

A NOTE: Some people use white granulated sugar in Caipirinhas, and it doesn't taste bad at all. I picked up the brown sugar tip from Dale DeGroff's *The Craft of the Cocktail*, and I like its more tropical nature. Feel free to play around with your sugars.

silk stocking

Add a little 1920s risqué flavor to an evening soirée with this brazen beauty of a cocktail. Like the attire its name borrows from, this luscious drink is smooth and may cause more than a little lightheadedness. But that's not always a bad thing, of course.

> **Ice cubes**
> **6 ounces white tequila**
> **6 ounces crème de cacao**
> **4 ounces heavy cream**
> **Ground cinnamon**

1. Fill a medium-size pitcher half full with ice cubes. Add the tequila, crème de cacao, and cream, together, while no one's looking (or behind a diaphanous dressing screen). Stir lovingly.

2. Pour the mix carefully into 4 martini glasses, making sure that no ice from the pitcher goes into the glasses.

3. Sprinkle a little ground cinnamon lightly on top of each drink. Serve with a knowing grin.

➤ A Variation: If you really want to turn up the heat, or have a special Valentine's treat, float a couple of heart-shaped cinnamon red hots on top of each drink.

SERVES 4

kir royale

This snazzy drink has a majestic sense about it. Have partygoers in tuxes and glittering gowns, betting C-notes (could be Monopoly money—but who cares?) over hotly contested hands of baccarat and talking about Matisse when serving and succumbing to the Kir Royale's charms. To reduce time and hassle once the evening's entertaining has begun, it's a good idea to pre-slice lemon twists for the inevitable second and third round of drinks.

4 ounces Framboise
One 750-milliliter bottle chilled Champagne
Lemon twists for garnish

1. Add 1 ounce Framboise to each of 4 Champagne flutes.
2. Fill the flutes with Champagne. Garnish each with a lemon twist.

SERVES 4

A NOTE: Framboise is a raspberry-flavored brandy. If you can't find it, go with Chambord (a raspberry-flavored liqueur) or crème de cassis, a lovely black currant–flavored liqueur often used in the Kir Royale with tasty results. And don't take any guff about it.

> "MY ONLY REGRET IN LIFE IS THAT I DID NOT DRINK MORE CHAMPAGNE."
> —JOHN MAYNARD KEYNES

mint julep

I would cry a Kentucky river to have to go through a Derby day, the first Saturday in May, without a Mint Julep. Even if you aren't a horse-racing fan, you'll find that spring and Mint Juleps were born to be together. Before making a Mint Julep, pause and remember that, as S.B. Buckner, Jr., told General Connor in 1937, "A Mint Julep is not the product of a formula. It is a ceremony and must be performed by a gentleman possessing a true sense of the artistic, a deep reverence for the ingredients, and a proper appreciation of the occasion." Make everyone wear an enormous hat and you'll be on your way to bringing the Derby home.

Fresh mint leaves (4 is a good number)
1 ounce Simple Syrup (page 13)
Crushed ice (whether you crush the ice in a cloth bag, as is traditional,
    is up to you)
3 ounces Kentucky bourbon
Fresh mint sprigs

1. If you have a metal julep cup, use it, of course. If not, use a highball glass. Take 1 mint leaf and rub it, by hand, over the inside of the glass, not missing an inch. Drop the leaf into the bottom of the glass when finished.

2. Add the rest of the mint leaves and the simple syrup to the glass. Using a muddler or a wooden spoon, muddle the mint leaves with the syrup vigorously, but with reverence.

3. Fill the glass half full with crushed ice. Add the bourbon. Stir well, until you notice the glass getting icy.

4. Fill the glass the rest of the way with crushed ice. Stir once. Garnish with sprigs of fresh mint.

SERVES 1

A NOTE: Unlike most of the drinks in this book, this recipe is built for one, because the preparation of a Mint Julep is a historic event, and making more than one at once will dull your appreciation of the moment a bit too much. But there's no need to try and share one Julep amongst a crowd. Just be sure to have enough ingredients for all.

mojito

This Cuban concoction has really spiced up bar menus over the past five years, becoming a fast favorite during the hotter months and festivals celebrating hard-drinking writer Ernest Hemingway (who fluctuated between Mojitos and Daiquiris when vacationing in Cuba in the early twentieth century). The rum base and fresh mint turn any backyard BBQ into a revolutionary affair—just be sure the mint is fresh, or the revolution may be to overthrow you.

Fresh mint leaves
2 lime quarters
1 ounce Simple Syrup (page 13)
Crushed ice
2 ½ ounces light rum
Club soda

1. Add a good bit of mint (at least 8 leaves), the lime quarters, and the simple syrup to a highball glass. Muddle well with a muddler or wooden spoon.

2. Fill the glass three quarters full with crushed ice. Add the rum while humming the Cuban national anthem (the anthem is optional).

3. Top off with club soda. Stir well.

SERVES 1

A NOTE: While this recipe is built for one (to focus in on the pleasure and necessity of the muddling), you'll want to be sure to have enough ingredients on hand for a crowd. If you'd like to make Mojitos by the pitcher, just be sure to keep the ratios intact between rum and simple syrup. Add enough mint and lime wedges and muddle, muddle, muddle.

flowered wine spritzer

This straightforward recipe impresses at spring garden soirées or at any other get-together where the guests are lounging outside, perhaps wearing attractive floral hats and cream-colored loafers. To make a successful spritzer, use white wine with a floral or fruity overtone, and one that's not too dry (Chardonnay is great, of course). Edible flowers are available in floral shops (make sure they haven't been treated with anything) and gourmet food stores—call in advance to be sure. Keep guests healthy—consult a flower professional before using random flowers blooming in your backyard.

16 ounces chilled white wine
14 ounces chilled club soda
1 cup edible flowers

1. Add 4 ounces wine to each of four 8-ounce flutes.
2. Add 3½ ounces club soda to each of the flutes.
3. Add ¼ cup flowers to each flute. With a stirring spoon, give each glass a gentle stir. Serve and watch the appreciation grow.

➤ A Variation: All right, we all realize that edible flowers aren't always available (though they make a stunning presentation when they are). Spritzers also work well with certain fruits. Dropping two or three frozen raspberries into each glass looks exquisite and keeps everything cool. Frozen strawberries also work well, and if you want to get fancier, add a strawberry slice to each glass as a garnish. You'll be toasted as elegant and urbane and be the first person picked to play croquet.

SERVES 4

"WINE IS SUNLIGHT, HELD TOGETHER BY WATER."
—GALILEO

gin stinger

Okay, we know Mr. Bond drinks Martinis, but other drinks also have that scent of secret agent. For me, the Gin Stinger is one of them. The name has a taste of danger, while the drink itself combines a creamy touch with always smooth gin.

Ice cubes
8 ounces gin
4 ounces white crème de menthe

1. Fill a cocktail shaker half full with ice cubes. Add the gin and crème de menthe. Shake vigorously, but cautiously.
2. Strain equally into 4 cocktail glasses and serve.

SERVES 4

A NOTE: Be careful when picking up your crème de menthe—you'll want white, not green.

ANOTHER NOTE: You can easily scale this back if you're making drinks for two secret agents. Just be sure to keep the ratio at 2 parts gin to 1 part white crème de menthe.

the rebecca

The key to The Rebecca is the raspberry. Lovable, with a light tang hiding beneath the kiss, it requires that you use raspberries that have been freshly picked, gently washed, carefully dried, and quickly frozen. Once you freeze the raspberries, they'll keep for a while without losing sweetness. They also keep the other ingredients chilled and are a bonus once they finally slip into your (and your guests') waiting mouth after the drink is finished.

> Ice cubes
> 8 ounces vodka (if you happen to have raspberry-infused vodka, all the better)
> 4 ounces Chambord or other raspberry liqueur
> Frozen raspberries
> 8 ounces Champagne

1. Add some ice cubes to your favorite cocktail shaker. Then, with care, add the vodka.

2. Add the Chambord. Shake. Shake. Shake.

3. Place 4 or 5 frozen raspberries into each of 4 martini glasses. Don't they look lovely? Strain the vodka and Chambord into the glasses over the raspberries.

4. Top off each drink with 2 ounces Champagne. Pour slowly so the Champagne just rests on top of the vodka/Chambord mix. Serve and drink and enjoy.

SERVES 4

A NOTE: This recipe is for a 5- to 6-ounce martini glass, but it can be adjusted accordingly if you have differently sized glasses. Just be sure to keep the ratio of 2 parts vodka to 1 part Chambord to 2 parts Champagne.

quenching the
multitudes

A mass of friends trudging toward your door? A host of folks descending on your den? A multitude of family members balancing on your balcony? Have no fear— this chapter's punches, nogs, and libations were designed for party posses of at least 10. Just fill up that oversized pitcher or punch bowl with the right mixture, set out a bunch of glasses, and start pouring. More guests just means more chances to amaze them, and the following oversized cocktails ensure that the party's going to be a huge success.

- Excellent Eggnog
- Gin Daisy
- Steaming Spiked Cider
- Christmas Punch
- Don't Just Stand There
- Her Sarong Slipped
- Hot Buttered Rum
- Italian Valium
- Hurricane
- Planter's Punch
- Sangria
- Champagne Punch

excellent eggnog

Whether you believe the word "eggnog" comes from the English "noggin" (a small glass with an upright handle) or from a combination of "egg" and "grog," chances are you've had this holiday special at Christmas, Thanksgiving, New Year's, or some other celebratory occasion. And with good reason—Eggnog is naturally festive, looks lovely, and tastes even better. It does take a little time to make, but it's worth it and always crowd-pleasing. Luckily, unlike some old Eggnog recipes, the following doesn't call for milking a cow straight into the mix. That shaves off prep time.

8 large eggs
2$\frac{1}{4}$ cups superfine sugar
8 ounces brandy
8 ounces light rum
4 ounces bourbon
1 quart milk
Freshly grated nutmeg

1. Separate the egg yolks from the egg whites, setting the whites aside for a moment.

2. In a good-size mixing bowl, beat the yolks with an electric mixer or whisk until they're completely combined. Add the sugar and beat until the mixture reaches a creamy consistency.

3. Add the brandy, rum, and bourbon, then the milk, beating well after each addition.

4. In another good-sized mixing bowl, beat the egg whites with an electric mixer until soft peaks form. (Be sure before beating the whites that the beaters have been cleaned and dried.) Fold the egg whites into the yolk-sugar-booze mixture—"fold" means don't mix it in like a wild person. Cover tightly and refrigerate the mix until well chilled, probably at least 3 hours or even overnight.

5. Serve the Eggnog in mugs, topping each with some freshly grated nutmeg.

➤ A Virgin Variation: For Angelic Eggnog, omit the rum, brandy, and bourbon. Add 2 ounces vanilla extract and $\frac{1}{4}$ cup heavy cream to the milk in step 3.

SERVES 10

A WARNING: While Eggnog is a tasty holiday treat, don't forget that it contains raw eggs. This means that it shouldn't be served to guests who are elderly or have compromised immune systems. Also, be doubly sure that you use completely fresh eggs and that this drink stays refrigerated during the party.

gin daisy

Don't be bamboozled (or let your guests be bamboozled) by this old favorite's flowery title—it packs a gin punch. Luckily, one of the hallmarks of the drink is that it's served in a mug with a handle, so there's always something solid to hold on to. This drink is great for large groups at large parties that are going to involve lots of toasting, which is why I like to serve this to at least 10 people. When you're holding a sturdy mug, the chance of inadvertent breakage during toasting decreases greatly.

Ice cubes
6 ounces fresh lemon juice
8 ounces Simple Syrup (page 13)
24 ounces gin
4 ounces grenadine
Maraschino cherries for garnish
Orange slices for garnish (optional)

1. Add two ice cubes each to 10 glass mugs (or other mug-type cup—make sure there's a handle).

2. Fill a pitcher halfway with ice cubes. Add the lemon juice, simple syrup, gin, and grenadine, in that order. Stir well.

3. Using your stirrer to hold back the ice in the pitcher, strain the mix equally into the mugs. Garnish each with a cherry. If a cherry solo seems lonely, also add an orange slice to each mug. If that still seems lonely, add another cherry. You see where this is leading.

SERVES 10

steaming
spiked cider

Cold evenings and holiday gatherings twinkle with this delight. It warms the belly and fills the room with a nice apple-cinnamon scent, pulling any party into the kitchen where it belongs. A thick and cloudy farm-fresh cider (not a hard or bubbly cider) works best, and you should have 10 or more cinnamon sticks available to put in the mugs when serving. Adding apple slices is another nice touch.

> **4 quarts fresh apple cider (the cloudier the better)**
> **16 ounces white rum**
> **20 ounces cinnamon schnapps**
> **1 teaspoon whole cloves**
> **³/₄ teaspoon freshly grated nutmeg**
> **Cinnamon sticks to taste**
> **Apple slices for garnish (optional)**

1. Pour the cider into a large nonreactive saucepan, turn the heat to medium, and let the cider warm for about 5 minutes.

2. Add the remaining ingredients except the garnish. Bring the heat up to just below boiling, and let it simmer for 15 minutes. You want it piping warm, but not so hot that it burns a guest's mouth.

3. Ladle into large heatproof mugs, adding a cinnamon stick or two to each mug, and an apple slice, if desired.

➤ A Virgin Variation: It's easy enough to make a saucepan of Nonalcoholic Steaming Cider to cater to the kids and nondrinking guests. Just leave out the rum and schnapps and add an extra ¼ cup cider and 1 ounce cinnamon extract (available in most grocery stores).

SERVES 10

A NOTE: It's nice to make enough so that a good amount stays warming on the stove. The aroma adds a festive smell, and the second mug, after the cider's flavors have really had time to get acquainted, tastes even better than the first. It's also easy to double this recipe or scale it back as needed. But no matter how much you make, err on the side of moderation with the cloves, as their flavor can take over the cider if you're not careful. If you feel the need to give the cider a bit more kick after it has cooked for a while, don't be afraid to add a little more rum.

christmas punch

Whether you love or despise the traditional December holiday season, it's one of the definitive times of year to celebrate or communally drown sorrows over a large, bubbling punch bowl. Christmas Punch is concocted differently from house to house, but it's best to set a few rules before pouring in shots off every bottle hiding near the back of the liquor cabinet. First, always have as a final and feature ingredient at least one bottle of Champagne. Any punch with Champagne in it is bound to be a hit. Second, especially during the colder months, make sure some sort of citrus fruit is involved (both to bring in a little sunshine and to guard against colds and scurvy). Third, stop adding different liquors when you get to four. More than four is almost inevitably asking for trouble, from both the perspective of taste and the possibility of a head-shattering hangover the next day. As with the Champagne Punch (page 92), put this together right before serving it.

> Ice (in block form if possible; if not, large chunks)
> 4 ounces Cointreau
> 4 ounces brandy
> 2 oranges, cut into wedges
> Two 750-milliliter bottles chilled Champagne

1. Add the ice to a large punch bowl. If using chunks (as opposed to a large block of ice), fill the bowl just less than halfway.
2. Add the Cointreau and brandy. Swirl around the ice.
3. Add the orange wedges, then slowly pour in the Champagne. Let everything mingle for 5 minutes. Serve in goblets.
➤ A Variation: If you feel the above recipe isn't quite festive enough, add 1 cup frozen cranberries to the bowl along with the Champagne.

SERVES 10

A NOTE: This recipe can easily serve less than 10, if they're a hardy bunch of holiday revelers. It could also serve more. If you have a large punch bowl, feel free to expand the recipe, adding another 2 ounces each of Cointreau and brandy for every added bottle of Champagne.

don't just stand there

I rescued this lovely concoction from Crosby Gaige's amazing *Cocktail Guide and Ladies' Companion*. If you can find that 1940s book, get it. Every party you throw from then on is guaranteed to generate congratulatory conversations for months. The dancing alone will be worth at least a month's (probably hushed) conversations. Supposedly, according to the book, this recipe comes from a Mr. Robert S. Allison Jr., who said, "Here is the recipe that made Aunt Dinah's quilting parties such a success." Who knew quilting could be so much fun? I've made minor modifications, but the theme mirrors the original.

Ice cubes
One 750-milliliter bottle sparkling (nonalcoholic) apple cider
One 750-milliliter bottle applejack

1. Fill a large pitcher with ice cubes.
2. Add the cider to the pitcher until it reaches the halfway mark.
3. Add the applejack until the pitcher is full. Stir with a large attractive spoon (just because).
4. Pour into as many highball glasses as there are people in the room.

SERVES 10

A NOTE: If you're feeling adventurous, garnish each glass with an apple slice.

her sarong
slipped

There are drinks whose origins inexplicably become lost in cocktail history. It's hard to believe that this is one of them—not only because it's a gorgeous, sparkling treat, but also because the name is so intriguingly naughty. You need to have whole parties organized around this drink. The invitations alone will draw larger crowds than expected, so have extra Champagne on hand, chilled.

> **Ice cubes**
> **4 ounces fresh lemon juice**
> **12 ounces brandy**
> **3 ounces grenadine**
> **One 750-milliliter bottle chilled Champagne**
> **Strawberry slices for garnish**

1. Fill a large pitcher half full with ice cubes. Add the lemon juice, brandy, and grenadine, in that order. Stir well.

2. Strain the mix equally into 10 white wine glasses (or comparable stemmed glasses).

3. Top off each glass with Champagne. Garnish each glass with a strawberry slice and serve with stirrers (if possible—if not, give each glass a quick stir before serving).

SERVES 10

hot buttered rum

This'll cure what ails you. When cold weather starts chilling the bones, don't reach for an extra sweater; instead, reach for the phone, invite over some friends, and have them pick up some rum and cider en route (and butter, if you're butter-deficient). While they're rounding up the supplies, you can start warming the mugs.

20 ounces dark rum
5 ounces Simple Syrup (page 13)
1 quart apple cider
2½ sticks (20 tablespoons) unsalted butter
1 quart boiling water
Cinnamon sticks for garnish
Freshly grated nutmeg for garnish

1. Add 2 ounces rum and ½ ounce simple syrup each to 10 sturdy 12-ounce heatproof mugs. Fill the mugs halfway with cider.

2. Add a 2-tablespoon pat of butter to each mug. Fill the mugs with boiling water.

3. Garnish each mug with a cinnamon stick (which will double as a stirrer) and some nutmeg.

SERVES 10

"THERE'S NOUGHT, NO DOUBT,
SO MUCH THE SPIRIT CALMS
AS RUM AND TRUE RELIGION."
—LORD BYRON

italian valium

When T.S. Eliot wrote, in "The Waste Land," "April is the cruellest month," he never knew his phrase would ring true annually for many Americans. The gloom of doing taxes (and the potential check-writing thereafter) leads whole crowds to sporting dour looks up to, on, and after April 15. But there is a way to combat this community depression, and that's by introducing the Italian Valium to all comers at your next tax-relief party (a type of party I find everyone needs in April—U.S. citizens or not). As far as I have ascertained, this shot originated in Auntie Mae's Parlor in Manhattan, Kansas, a bar that is almost 90 percent underground. Perhaps only in a bar that is so bereft of daylight would the bartenders think of mixing Amaretto and Crown Royal to chase away the April blues.

Ice cubes
10 ounces Amaretto
10 ounces Crown Royal

1. Fill a cocktail shaker half full with ice cubes. Pour the Amaretto and Crown Royal simultaneously into the shaker, even if the Crown (or the crowd) seems unhappy with the idea.
2. Shake well and quickly. Strain the mix into 10 shot glasses or any short, wide-mouthed glass. Instruct participants to drink in one fluid motion.

SERVES 10

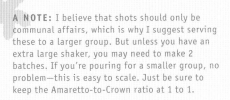

A NOTE: I believe that shots should only be communal affairs, which is why I suggest serving these to a larger group. But unless you have an extra large shaker, you may need to make 2 batches. If you're pouring for a smaller group, no problem—this is easy to scale. Just be sure to keep the Amaretto-to-Crown ratio at 1 to 1.

hurricane

A New Orleans favorite, this drink rapidly livens up an evening (just don't down too many, or you'll feel as if an actual hurricane blew through your brain). It's tropical and, when made right, not overly sugary. I like to serve it as a punch, because no one wants to ride out a hurricane alone. If you have actual Hurricane glasses (nine-inch-tall glasses with a bulbous middle and a smaller outward curve at the top), then use them—but if not, don't let that stop you. You can still have your very own Mardi Gras.

Ice (in block form, if possible; if not, large chunks)
4 ounces fresh lime juice
4 ounces pineapple juice
2 ounces passion fruit syrup
2 ounces grenadine
12 ounces light rum
4 ounces dark rum
Ice cubes
Orange slices for garnish

1. Add the ice to a large punch bowl. If using chunks (as opposed to a large block of ice), fill the bowl just less than halfway.

2. Add the juices, syrup, and grenadine. With a large spoon or ladle, stir the mix until the ingredients have become acquainted.

3. Add the rums. With a large spoon or ladle, stir the mix a second time.

4. Ladle the drink into large glasses that have been filled three quarters full with ice cubes. Garnish each with an orange slice and an umbrella (it sometimes rains during a hurricane).

SERVES 10

A NOTE: Passion fruit syrup can be hard to find (try a gourmet food store). If you absolutely can't track it down, substitute 2 ounces Simple Syrup (page 13) and a lotta love.

planter's punch

There are almost as many Planter's Punch variations as Bloody Mary recipes (though no blows get thrown over Planter's Punch—except maybe in Miami). The two constants in the P.P. are lots of rum and pineapple juice. I suppose any cocktail with abundant ingredients breeds variations, but let me say assuredly and modestly that the following is the finest of all the recipes out there. Planter's Punch is best served after a long day of work in the yard or garden. Or, possibly, after a long day of thinking about working in the yard or garden.

Ice (in block form if possible; if not, large chunks)
20 ounces dark rum
5 ounces fresh lime juice
2½ ounces fresh lemon juice
20 ounces fresh orange juice
20 ounces pineapple juice
5 ounces Simple Syrup (page 13)
8 dashes Angostura bitters
Ice cubes
Orange slices and pineapple chunks for garnish

1. Add the ice to a large punch bowl. If using chunks (as opposed to a large block of ice), fill the bowl just less than halfway.

2. Add all the ingredients to the bowl, except the garnishes, quickly, as if being chased. Stir the mix well with a long spoon or pitchfork.

3. Fill 10 goblets three quarters full with ice cubes, then fill with the punch. Garnish each with an orange slice and a couple of pineapple chunks (float them on top).

➤ A Variation: Well, as mentioned, there are many. Some like to add a splash of grapefruit juice, which brings a little tang to the soirée. Others omit the bitters and lemon juice. Also, you could add 2 ounces club soda to each goblet after the punch is poured (adding a little less punch than above, naturally).

SERVES 10

sangria

Sangria may be the drink I fear most when ordering at a bar or restaurant. Too often pitchers are made far in advance and left to "mature" for weeks at a time. Which is a shame, because pitchers of Sangria are the perfect accompaniment to a spicy Mexican or Spanish feast—a true match made in culinary heaven. So instead of getting the Sangria shaft at a local eatery, serve it at home, where it'll be the fiesta highlight.

    1 orange, cut into wheels
    1 lime, cut into wheels
    1 lemon, cut into wheels
    10 ounces Simple Syrup (page 13)
    6 ounces fresh orange juice
    4 ounces fresh lime juice
    One 750-milliliter bottle dry red wine
    8 ounces brandy
    Ice cubes
    Other sliced fresh fruit for garnish (oranges, limes, lemons, apples)

1. Place the orange, lime, and lemon wheels in a large glass pitcher, along with the simple syrup. Muddle well with a large muddler or wooden spoon.

2. Add the orange juice and lime juice and muddle a little more.

3. Add the wine and brandy and stir well for 15 seconds. Place the pitcher in the refrigerator for up to several hours, even overnight, covering the top if you wish.

4. When ready to serve, add ice cubes until the pitcher is full. Give the mix a couple of good stirs. Pour into 10 wine glasses. Garnish with fresh fruit.

➤ A Variation: White Sangria is also tasty and easy to make. Substitute dry white wine for the red, 3 ounces white grape juice for the lime juice, and 1 cored, peeled, and sliced apple for the lime in the above recipe.

SERVES 10

champagne punch

As with any punch, there are numerous variations on this one. In one old bartenders guide, for example, I found eight. So you have some liberty here, but much like with Christmas Punch (page 82), follow some rules. Always serve this in a classy punch bowl. Always add the Champagne last. Always follow the four-liquor rule.

I like to use the following recipe in the summer (the rum season) or on temperate spring and fall Saturdays. Serving a Champagne punch outside turns any gathering into an elegant affair. This should be put together right before you are ready to serve it—Champagne Punch waits for no man.

> Ice (in block form if possible; if not, large chunks)
> 6 ounces fresh orange juice
> 2 ounces fresh lime juice
> 2 ounces fresh lemon juice
> 4 ounces Simple Syrup (page 13)
> 6 ounces light rum
> 6 ounces dark rum
> One 750-milliliter bottle chilled Champagne
> Orange, lime, and lemon slices for garnish

1. Add the ice to a large punch bowl. If using chunks (as opposed to a large block of ice), fill the bowl just less than halfway.

2. Add the juices and the simple syrup. With a large spoon or ladle, swirl the mix. Add the rums. With the same large spoon or ladle, swirl the mix a second time.

3. Add the Champagne, carefully, but with an illusion of a devil-may-care attitude. Give a final gentle swirl.

4. Serve in punch glasses, or other goblet-esque glasses, garnishing each with slices of orange, lime, and lemon.

➤ A Virgin Variation: Okay, it may seem odd to have a virgin-style "Champagne" punch, but it's a good idea and relatively simple. Omit the rum, increase the orange juice to 12 ounces, the lime and lemon juices to 3 ounces each, and the Simple Syrup to 6 ounces, and substitute one 2-liter bottle of chilled club soda for the Champagne.

SERVES 10

index

measurement equivalents

Please note that all conversions are approximate.

U.S./U.K.	METRIC
1 teaspoon	5 ml
1 tablespoon	15 ml
1 fl. oz.	30 ml
2 fl. oz.	60 ml
2½ fl. oz.	75 ml
4 fl. oz.	120 ml
5 fl. oz.	150 ml
6 fl. oz.	180 ml
8 fl. oz.	240 ml
10 fl. oz.	300 ml
12 fl. oz.	360 ml
1 pint (16 fl. oz.)	480 ml
1 quart (32 fl. oz.)	960 ml

about the author

A.J. Rathbun is a kitchen, house-wares, and entertainment editor for Amazon.com. Since earning his MFA in creative writing from Western Michigan University, Rathbun has worked as a bartender, usher at the Art Institute of Chicago, rock band roadie, envelope stuffer, marketing assistant, and waiter. He is the author of *Want*, a collection of poems, and co-editor of the literary magazine *LitRag*. He has hosted numerous poetry readings. A.J. lives in Seattle.

Photo by Sara Mahlin